The Let's Talk Library™

Let's Talk About
When Kids Have Cancer

Melanie Apel Gordon

The Rosen Publishing Group's

PowerKids Press™
New York

With love for Darwin R. Apel, my dad, in his fight. Love, Melanie

Published in 1999 by The Rosen Publishing Group, Inc.
29 East 21st Street, New York, NY 10010

First Edition

Book Design: Erin McKenna

Photo Illustrations: Cover photo © Telegraph Colour Library/FPG; pp. 4, 8, 15, 16, 19, 20 by Seth Dinnerman; p. 7 © J. L. Carson/Custom Medical Stock Photo; p. 11 © K. Glaser and Associates/ Custom Medical Stock Photo; p. 12 by Carrie Grippo.

Gordon, Melanie Apel.
    Let's talk about when kids have cancer / by Melanie Apel Gordon.
        p.   cm. — (The Let's talk library)
    Includes index.
    Summary: Discusses what cancer is, its treatment and side effects, and how it affects the lives of its victims and their families.
    ISBN 0-8239-5195-2
    1. Cancer—Juvenile literature. 2. Tumors in children—Juvenile literature. [1. Cancer.] I. Title. II. Series.
RC264.G67 1998
616.99'4—dc21   97-38704
                                                                            CIP
                                                                             AC

Manufactured in the United States of America

Table of Contents

Dylan and Isabella

Dylan and his friend Isabella are excited. They are going to camp. For a week they will share a cabin with friends, ride horses, and go fishing. But the thing that Dylan and Isabella like best about camp is that they will be just like everyone else there. Like Dylan and Isabella, all of their friends at camp have **cancer** (KAN-ser). Some of their friends are thin. Some are bald. They have to take **medicine** (MED-ih-sin), and they know what it's like to be in the hospital.

◀ Kids with cancer like to do the same things as kids who don't have cancer.

5

What Is Cancer?

Your body is made up of millions of **cells** (SELZ). Each cell has a job. When a cell gets old, it splits into two copies of itself. The copies do the same job that the old cell did. But sometimes cells grow and split too fast, and the new copies don't work right. These are cancer cells.

When lots of cancer cells clump together they make a **tumor** (TOO-mer). When cancer cells get in the way of healthy cells, you get sick.

This blown-up photo shows what cancer cells look like. ▶

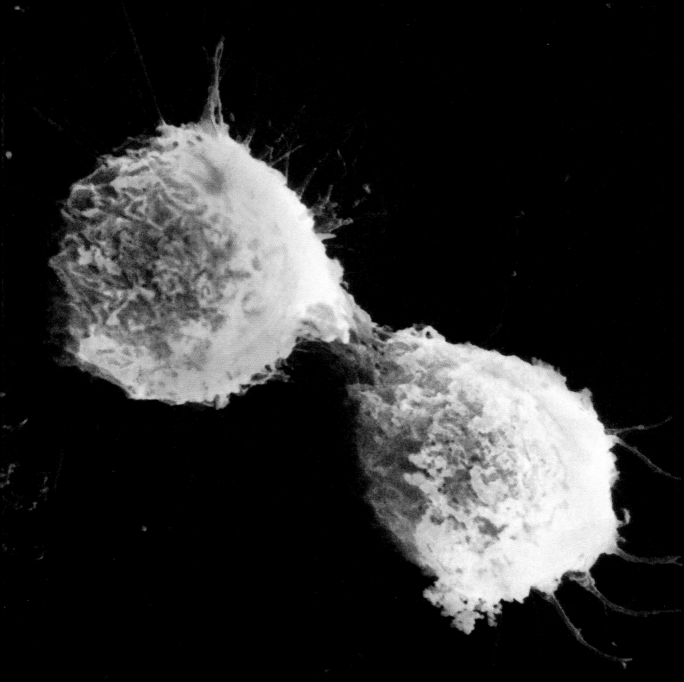

Ana Is Sick

When Ana goes into the hospital she brings comic books, her stuffed dog Puddles, and her favorite pajamas. Ana's class at school makes her cards and pictures. Her mom helps her hang them on the walls in her hospital room.

Ana's mom and dad take turns spending the night with her in the hospital. Doctors and nurses take care of Ana and try to make her cancer go away.

◀ If you have cancer, you may have to stay in the hospital for a long time. It might make you feel better to hang up the cards and pictures that your friends and family send to you.

Fighting Cancer

Most kids with cancer are given medicine called **chemotherapy** (KEE-moh-THER-uh-pee) to fight their cancer. The medicine drips into their arms through an **IV** (EYE VEE).

Even though the medicine helps fight cancer, it hurts some of the healthy cells in their bodies too. And it can make kids feel sick. Chemotherapy can also make your hair fall out. Some kids wear cool hats or scarves until their hair grows back.

Even though chemotherapy can make you feel sick, it is working to help your body. ▶

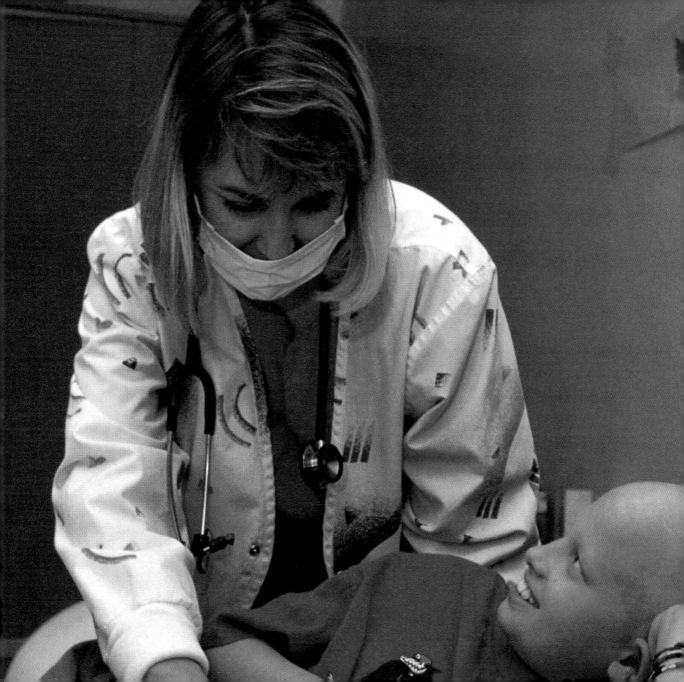

Surgery and Radiation

Some kids have **surgery** (SER-juh-ree) to take out their tumors. Some kids have a treatment called **radiation** (ray-dee-AY-shun). Radiation is a kind of energy that is pointed right at the tumor. It shrinks the tumor until it's all gone.

The **radiologist** (ray-dee-AHL-uh-jist) draws dots on your body so he knows where to aim the radiation. You have to lie very still on a table while you get radiation treatments. Radiation usually does not make you feel sick.

◄ Ask your doctor to explain your treatment to you. This way you will know what to expect.

How Do People Get Cancer?

We don't know all the reasons why people get cancer. But we do know that you can't catch cancer from somebody who has it. Things that cause cancer are called **carcinogens** (kar-SIN-uh-jenz).

To help **prevent** (pre-VENT) cancer, stay away from carcinogens such as cigarettes, certain chemicals, fatty foods, and too much sun. It is also important to exercise and take good care of your body.

14

Eating healthy foods can help prevent cancer. ▶

Who Gets Cancer?

Anyone can get cancer. Grown-ups, old people, kids, and even babies can get cancer. Young and old people who are **exposed** (eks-POHZD) to carcinogens are more likely to get cancer than people who are not. But older people are more likely to get cancer than kids. In fact, only one out of every 10,000 kids gets cancer.

◀ Kids with cancer can still do most of the things that they enjoy.

Feelings

Having cancer is scary. Sometimes kids and their families cry when the doctor says they have cancer. Kids with cancer and their sisters or brothers often will talk to a **counselor** (KOWN-suh-ler) about their feelings. Brothers and sisters may feel upset because the sick person gets so much attention. They may be angry that someone they love has cancer. Or they may be afraid that person will die. It's okay to be afraid or mad. People with cancer wish they weren't sick. They are afraid too.

Talking about your feelings with a grown-up ▶
or a counselor can make you feel better.

Back to School

When Sam gets out of the hospital, he goes back to school. He and his parents talk about how to tell the kids in his class that he is sick. At school Sam tells his class that he has cancer. The kids ask questions. He tells them that chemotherapy makes him feel sick. He tells them all about the hospital and about radiation. He wants his classmates to know that they can't catch cancer from him. And even though he is sick he's still their friend Sam.

◀ Kids with cancer can talk to their friends to help them understand the illness.

21

What Happens Next?

Some kids go into **remission** (ree-MISH-un) after radiation or chemotherapy. Remission is when the doctor can't find any more cancer in a person's body. If the cancer doesn't come back in a certain number of years—usually five—then the doctor says that the person is cured. If the cancer comes back, then he or she has to fight it again. But sometimes cancer can't be cured and sometimes people die. Doctors and scientists are working very hard to keep kids with cancer alive and healthy.

Glossary

cancer (KAN-ser) A disease in which cells keep growing and splitting but do not work properly.

carcinogen (kar-SIN-uh-jen) Something that causes cancer.

cell (SEL) One of many tiny units that make up your body.

chemotherapy (KEE-moh-THER-uh-pee) Medicine that fights cancer.

counselor (KOWN-suh-ler) Someone to talk to about your feelings and problems.

expose (eks-POHZ) To be near something.

IV (EYE VEE) A tube that allows medicine to flow directly into your body—usually through your arm.

medicine (MED-ih-sin) Drugs that help your body fight illness.

prevent (pre-VENT) To keep something from happening.

radiation (ray-dee-AY-shun) Energy that doctors use to shrink tumors.

radiologist (ray-dee-AHL-uh-jist) A doctor who gives radiation treatments.

remission (ree-MISH-un) When no more cancer is found in the body.

surgery (SER-juh-ree) An operation.

tumor (TOO-mer) A mass of cancer cells.

Index